# The Art of Peer Coaching

# The Art of Peer Coaching

## A Practical Manual for Teachers

Lanette Bridgman

ROWMAN & LITTLEFIELD
*Lanham • Boulder • New York • London*

Published by Rowman & Littlefield
An imprint of The Rowman & Littlefield Publishing Group, Inc.
4501 Forbes Boulevard, Suite 200, Lanham, Maryland 20706
www.rowman.com

6 Tinworth Street, London SE11 5AL, United Kingdom

Copyright © 2020 by Lanette Bridgman

*All rights reserved.* No part of this book may be reproduced in any form or by any electronic or mechanical means, including information storage and retrieval systems, without written permission from the publisher, except by a reviewer who may quote passages in a review.

British Library Cataloguing in Publication Information Available

**Library of Congress Cataloging-in-Publication Data**

Names: Bridgman, Lanette, 1953– author.
Title: The art of peer coaching : a practical manual
  for teachers / Lanette Bridgman.
Description: Lanham : Rowman & Littlefield, 2020. |
  Includes bibliographical references and index. |
  Summary: "The purpose of this book is to share with
  teachers a successful coaching model"—Provided by publisher.
Identifiers: LCCN 2020011157 (print) | LCCN 2020011158 (ebook) |
  ISBN 9781475857078 (cloth) | ISBN 9781475857085 (paperback) |
  ISBN 9781475857092 (epub)
Subjects: LCSH: Teachers—In-service training. | Peer review. |
  Mentoring in education.
Classification: LCC LB1731 .B7245 2020 (print) | LCC LB1731 (ebook) |
  DDC 370.71/1—dc23
LC record available at https://lccn.loc.gov/2020011157
LC ebook record available at https://lccn.loc.gov/2020011158

To all hard-working teachers,
this is for you.

# Contents

| | | |
|---|---|---|
| Preface | | ix |
| Acknowledgments | | xi |
| Introduction | | xiii |
| 1 | What Is Coaching? | 1 |
| 2 | Who Can Coach? | 3 |
| 3 | Who Can Be Coached? | 5 |
| 4 | Coaching Skills | 7 |
| 5 | Key Concepts within This Peer Coaching Framework | 13 |
| 6 | Possible Ideas for Coaching | 17 |
| 7 | Getting Started | 21 |
| 8 | The Process | 23 |
| 9 | Initial Interview | 25 |
| 10 | Observation | 31 |
| 11 | Follow-up Meeting | 39 |
| 12 | Next Steps | 45 |
| 13 | Case Study A | 49 |
| 14 | Case Study B | 63 |

| | | |
|---|---|---|
| **15** | Case Study C | 77 |
| **16** | Case Study D | 87 |

| | |
|---|---|
| References | 103 |
| Index | 105 |
| About the Author | 107 |

# Preface

Teaching is at the heart of my being. After thirty-five years in education, having taught and worked with students aged five to sixteen years old, mentored student teachers, coached and supported teachers, taken on a variety of roles in education, I decided it was time to give something back. Hence, *The Art of Peer Coaching: A Practical Manual for Teachers* is that gift. Teaching is an art, coaching is an art, peer coaching is an art. Teaching isn't easy, and no matter how many years of experience we have, we can always learn new skills and improve the ones we have. Here is a safe environment that can be created to do just that.

# Acknowledgments

I would like to thank the many students I have taught and supported over the years. I'm sure they didn't know it at the time, and neither did I, but they taught me an enormous amount about "how to teach."

Thank you to all the teachers who allowed me into their classrooms. It was a privilege to be part of their own "world of teaching."

Finally, I am indebted to my husband and daughter, my "rocks," for their unending love and support.

# Introduction

As teachers, we are always learning. It doesn't matter if we are new to the profession or have years of experience. There is always something to learn! Sometimes it is what we teach; sometimes it is how we teach. Sometimes it is how children learn; sometimes it is how they interact with each other. But we do learn.

One way we can learn is through peer coaching.

And that is the purpose of this book: to share with teachers a successful coaching model that has been researched, designed, piloted, evaluated, and used across a range of schools, all ages.

It is a peer coaching model which teachers use with teachers. It is a model which, as a coach or coachee, you will learn from.

The model is respectful, confidential, and voluntary. It allows those being coached to have full ownership. It is positive and builds on the skills the teacher already possesses. It allows the coach to become the coachee and vice versa.

Possible areas for coaching may include: learning more about the teacher's subject matter, how to improve delivery of lessons, having an increased understanding of how children learn, being more effective in managing behavior, dealing with out-of-classroom duties such as meetings with parents and colleagues, or delivering training sessions. This peer coaching model can be used by classroom teachers, middle management, or school leaders.

The model leads to an increase in critical thinking, reflective learning, and self-coaching.

It is a cost-effective model as it does not need outside professionals to train staff. The book is clear and concise with relevant background information, a step-by-step process, and examples in the form of case studies.

This peer coaching model can easily be part of a menu of support for staff development so that teachers can use it on an "as –needed" basis.

While the model is designed for teachers, it is equally applicable and transferable to other professions, such as industry, commerce, sales, health, and public sector roles.

Below are some of the comments from teachers who have been coached using this model:

- "I felt supported."
- "I have more confidence."
- "The feedback from the observations was positive and constructive."
- "The confidentiality of the model was very important to me."
- "Having a process that was voluntary was empowering. It made me want to do it. Otherwise, it would have been a threat."
- "It was non-confrontational. I didn't feel pressured."
- "The questioning was good. It made me think."
- "It has opened up dialogue with myself and my peer which we find is on-going."
- "You recognize in yourself the progress you are making."
- "What I do now is a direct result of the observations and our meetings."
- "I am teaching more."
- "There is more learning."
- "I give more praise."
- "We have better relationships within the class."

Turn the page to find out more . . .

*Chapter 1*

# What Is Coaching?

People often interchange coaching with mentoring. Yes, there are *similarities* between the two, but there are key *differences* too.

It can be explained using a line of continuum with mentoring at one end and coaching at the other as shown in Figure 1.1. This recognizes the *similarities* between the two, as identified by the Centre for the Use of Research and Evidence in Education (CUREE, 2005: online):

Both are vehicles for analysis, reflection, and action that allow recipients to achieve success.

| Mentoring | Coaching |
|---|---|

**Figure 1.1.** The Line of Continuum from Mentoring to Coaching.

By contrast, consider that the *differences* between mentoring and coaching depend on the experience, performance, and, importantly, level of ownership of the recipient (MacLennan, 1995:4–6).

As such, mentoring would include the below:

- Shared ownership between the mentor and recipient.
- Goals set and agreed by mentor and recipient.
- Mentor guides recipient through a period of development and offers support, guidance, and expertise.
- Mentor is part of the process themselves.

At the opposite end of the continuum, coaching would include the below:

- Full ownership by recipient.
- Goals set by recipient.
- Coach works with recipient to achieve his/her potential as defined and directed by recipient.
- Coach stands back and facilitates the process.

The model described in this book is a coaching model, not a mentoring model.

As one moves from mentoring towards coaching, there is an increase in experience and performance and, essentially, control and ownership by the recipient. The skills of analyzing the situation, being able to critically reflect one's own practice, and taking appropriate action are necessary for growth to occur, whether in a mentoring or coaching situation.

Many teachers naturally self-coach (MacLennan, 1995:5), whether consciously or unconsciously. We reflect, we listen, and we watch other teachers; we think things through, we try new methods, we reassess, and we try again. Coaching is a cyclical process, whether we self-coach or are coached by others. In this sense, the coaching process will continue through self-coaching, consciously, even after it has formally ended.

There are other coaching models elsewhere that teachers can choose from. Many imply a more senior member of staff is coaching a less senior member. This coaching model is based on teacher-to-teacher support or peer coaching. It is about colleagues working collaboratively to solve their own classroom issues (Gottesman, 2000:5). There are specific skills and key concepts to this peer coaching model that are integral to its success and will be explained in full detail in the following chapters.

*Chapter 2*

# Who Can Coach?

Theoretically, anyone can coach. Some will be able to do it instinctively. Others will need to learn new skills. Realistically, some will be better at it than others. Some will find it a much more enjoyable and worthwhile experience. It is vital to note here that *bad coaching is worse than no coaching.*

Being a successful coach depends on his/her:

- attitude,
- skills,
- effort.

## ATTITUDE

*It is important that the coach is open to learning,* open to viewing things from a different stance, open to seeing a new mindset, and open to approaching things from a different position.

*The coach is non-judgmental.* The process isn't about being critical and finding fault; it is about leading the coachee to find the positives and explore new ways of problem solving through careful questioning.

*The coach is respectful at all times.* They honor the commitment made and follow through in a polite and courteous manner.

*The coach honors fully the agreement of confidentiality.* This is an important part of the process and key to its success. As long as the coach and coachee are safe, others are safe and there are no "disclosures," what is said in the meetings and/or observations remain between the two parties. This needs to be explicit at the start of the process.

*The coach follows the guidance of this model.* There are no surprises. Both parties, the coach and coachee, follow the protocol described in this book.

## SKILLS

The skills needed to coach, using this model, are understanding and implementing the following:

- How adults learn,
- Active listening skills,
- Socratic questioning,
- Pygmalion effect,
- Scaling,
- Johari Window.

Chapter 4, "Coaching Skills," will explain these six skills in detail, as they are very important to the process.

## EFFORT

Commitment, at all levels, is important:

- Being committed to the process,
- Being committed to the coachee,
- Being committed to oneself.

Coaching is no different, Whatever model is followed, coaching takes commitment, effort, and time in order to be successful.

A successful coach is one who has "knowledge and understanding of the process as well as the variety of styles, skills and techniques that are appropriate to the context in which the coaching takes place" (Parsloe and Wray, 2000:42).

*Chapter 3*

# Who Can Be Coached?

Someone with the same attitudes and effort as those previously described of a coach are the ones who can be coached successfully. It is why this model is ideal as a peer coaching model. It is about two teachers being involved in the process, one as a coach and the other as a coachee, and then the roles are swapped.

If someone's attitude is that of reflection, open-mindedness to new ideas, and a desire to continually improve one's expertise, then learning will take place and success will follow. Choice, motivation, and empowerment are an integral part of success. It takes effort. It takes time.

Asking for assistance is not a weakness. Instead, it is a strength. And coaching builds a deeper strength within us which improves our abilities as a teacher. Coaching builds our resilience too.

It is also worth knowing that not everyone is "ripe" for coaching. It is previously noted that mentoring is slightly different from coaching. A mentor is someone with a more senior role, who is experienced and able to impart knowledge, thus providing feedback and appraisal, as well as acting in a nurturing and supportive role (MacLennan, 1995:56). If someone needs greater support, guidance, and expertise, then a mentoring package would be more suitable. This would look different from coaching. A mentoring package may include the below:

- Discussions
- Sharing goal setting
- Frequent, brief one-to-one sessions
- Observations
- Feedback/recommendations given
- Modeling

- Team teaching
- Attending courses
- Reading relevant and recommended literature/books
- Keeping a professional daily journal
- Being part of a wider support network

This list is not exhaustive. As with coaching, it is offering support on an "as –needed" basis.

*Chapter 4*

# Coaching Skills

The following skills for a coach, mentioned in chapter 2, are fundamental to the success of this coaching model:

- How adults learn,
- Active listening skills,
- Socratic questioning,
- Pygmalion effect,
- Scaling,
- Johari Window.

Coaching is not simply a list of questions or procedures to go through. It is multilayered. There is background knowledge to this coaching model which is needed to be understood and acquired.

## HOW ADULTS LEARN

The following factors are key to understanding how adults learn and how they become engaged in the learning (Knowles, 1980, cited in Rhodes et al., 2004:51):

- Adults learn best when they are involved in diagnosing, planning, implementing, and evaluating their own learning.
- The role of the coach is to create and maintain a supportive climate that promotes the conditions necessary for learning to take place.
- Adult learners have a need to be self-directing.

- Readiness for learning increases when there is a specific need to know.
- Life's reservoir of experience is a primary learning resource and the life experiences of others add enrichment to the learning process.
- Adult learners have an inherent need for immediacy of application.
- Adults respond best to learning when they are internally motivated to learn.

Coaching is about learning in a real-life setting: the classroom. The learning becomes effective, and the experience generates knowledge that lasts and can be put into practice (Senge, 1999, cited in Fiszer, 2004:6).

This coaching model was described by a coachee in the following way: "The whole nature of the model is really to help the teacher. If a teacher can tailor it for themselves then they benefit the most and that has an impact."

## ACTIVE LISTENING SKILLS

There are verbal and nonverbal signs of listening. It is important that the coach is aware of body language, personal space, tone of voice, and manner. Guidelines include the below:

- Sit at an angle, look relaxed yet focused.
- Always allow the coachee to sit nearest to the door.
- Have paper and pencil ready for note-taking, but it should not distract the coach from listening intently.
- Use eye contact.
- Smile, nod.
- Don't be distracted.
- Reflect back what is being said.
- Paraphrase to show comprehension.
- Ask relevant questions for clarification and deeper thought.
- Allow for silence. Silence is powerful. It allows the coachee time to reflect and think.
- Summarize main points. Allow the coachee to correct if necessary.

## SOCRATIC QUESTIONING

Socratic questioning is a series of questions asked in order to enable the coachee to arrive at the desired understanding by themselves. It was Socrates's belief that conclusions we arrive at by our own critical thinking are more memorable to us than something which someone provides for us (MacLennan, 1995:66–67).

- Use open-ended questions to allow for much longer responses.
- Encourage further thought, again and again.
- Probe.
- Ask for evidence, viewpoint.
- Use phrases such as "tell me about," "tell me more," and "what are your ideas" and words such as "explain" and "how" (Rhodes et al., 2004:107–109).
- Encourage thinking, evaluating, analyzing.
- Periodically summarize key points.

Examples:

What is working successfully? What else? What else? What else?
It sounds likes you are saying . . .
Where is there a greater difficulty?
What are you hoping to improve upon?
Tell me more . . .
It sounds like you want to . . .
Have you considered . . .
What ideas do you have? What else? What else? What else?
Explain.
How?
It sounds like you are saying . . .
How can you achieve your goal? What else? What else? What else?
What will you notice? What else? What else? What else?
What will the student/s notice? What else? What else? What else?
What will others notice? What else? What else? What else?

## PYGMALION EFFECT

It is important to build on the coachee's positives so that self-esteem, self-awareness, and self-confidence are maintained and raised even higher. It is a critical part of the process (Parsloe and Wray, 2000:37). This is termed the "Pygmalion Effect," which says that the more belief one has in another individual, the more successful that second individual will be (Clutterbuck and Megginson, 2005:34).

The coach's aim is to help the coachee recognize what they can do and what is successful for them, to believe in their own abilities and to reflect on an area of difficulty in order to set a goal and to explore new ways of problem solving (Rhodes et al., 2004:119–20).

Examples:

This is what you said is working . . . And this . . . And this . . .
This is what you are doing successfully . . . And this . . . And this . . .
The students are achieving this . . . And this . . . And this . . .
Others have said (positives only) . . . And this . . . And this . . .
Others have seen (positives only) . . . And this . . . And this . . .

## SCALING

The scaling process used in this coaching model is from the world of psychotherapy, specifically the Solution-Focused Brief Therapy as developed by Steve de Shazer in the 1970s (George et al., 2006:2). The scale framework is flexible and is scored from 0 to 10. It offers 10 as being the "best" things could be. At the opposite end of this scale is 0, which represents the "worst" things could be.

The scaling process is used by the coachee to reflect on their initial situation and then repeatedly over time, based on the goals previously set by them. The rating is the coachee's own and is a subjective, rather than an objective, assessment. However, when ratings, included with their descriptions, are compared over a period of time, it is possible to see movement on the scale indicating the situation improving, getting worse, or remaining the same (George et al., 2006:16).

## JOHARI WINDOW

The Johari Window illustrates human behavior and the relationship one has with oneself and others. It was devised by Joseph Tuft and Harry Ingham in 1955 at UCLA, California (Wikipedia, 2006). Figure 4.1 represents the model of the Johari Window and, in this instance, its working relationship between coachee and coach (Luft, 1969, cited in De Haan and Burger, 2005:15; West, 1998:66–67; Rhodes et al., 2004:29–31).

The human behavior the Johari Window represents in coaching is the working relationship between coachee and coach in terms of classroom observations:

*Coaching Skills* 11

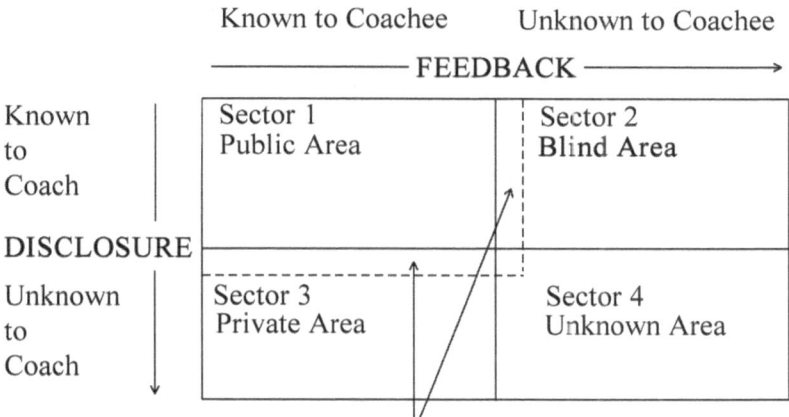

**Figure 4.1.** Model of Johari Window.

- It recognizes that there are parts of the coachee's behavior that will be known to them and to the coach. This is termed the "public area."
- It also recognizes that there is a "blind area." This is the area that will be known by the coach but not the coachee. It will be up to the coach to decide whether or not to share this with the coachee. This can be done through careful questioning, so that the coachee can discover the "blind area" for themselves, or the coach may decide to share the information explicitly. This sharing would extend the "public area."
- The "private area" is what is only known to the coachee. It can be disclosed and can become the public area if it is the coachee's wish.
- The "unknown area" is the unconscious territory which houses distant emotions, ideas, and memories which may surface later for the coachee and which neither the coachee nor coach can anticipate. The coach must remain aware of the power and process of the coaching conversations and the importance of being open-minded, being non-judgmental, and showing empathy.

If challenging emotions or memories surface for the coachee, then the coach must stop questioning and allow the coachee time to sit quietly. Time to rest. Time to reflect. Time to be still. Stay with the coachee, don't abandon them. Offer to get them a drink of water, tea, or coffee.

Once the situation neutralizes, ask the coachee what they would like to do next. They may want to continue with the meeting or they may want to reschedule and finish at another time. Don't let the situation "hang in the air."

Offer options. In addition, follow the school's protocol regarding pastoral care for staff. Offer any additional support, from their line manager, your line manager, senior staff, or even outside agencies.

It is important that both parties, the coach and the coachee, are being looked after.

Having a positive working relationship between coach and coachee is vital to the level of success that can be achieved through any type of coaching, in particular peer coaching.

*Chapter 5*

# Key Concepts within This Peer Coaching Framework

The key concepts of this peer coaching model have been identified through extensive reading, field research, and experience (Clutterbuck and Megginson, 2005; CUREE, 2005; MacLennan, 1995; Parsloe and Wray, 2000; The Coaching and Mentoring Network, 2006). It is important that these concepts are followed and incorporated fully in this model's peer coaching process:

- To provide a coaching model which is voluntary.
- To provide confidentiality.
- To establish a positive working relationship between the coach and coachee.
- To listen and to question skillfully.
- To observe carefully.
- To build on positives the coachee already possesses.
- To facilitate the change the coachee desires.
- To help the coachee find the skills to sustain that change.
- To recognize, as a coach, that one can learn from this process as well.

## TO PROVIDE A COACHING MODEL WHICH IS VOLUNTARY

It is vital that the teachers taking part in this coaching process, as a coach or coachee, are committed and have true ownership. In order for this to occur, it must be on a voluntary basis only. The sense of ownership is central to commitment and persistence and is an aspect of the most successful coaching models (MacLennan, 1995:60).

## TO PROVIDE CONFIDENTIALITY

Ensuring confidentiality by the coach is a fundamental step to embarking on this coaching process. It is important for the coachee to feel safe, to try new skills, to have the opportunity to make mistakes, and to learn from those mistakes. A safe atmosphere is best set by providing confidentiality. It will be up to the coachee to choose whether to share or discuss any successes with their colleagues. There is no mandate to do so.

The coach maintains confidentiality so long as the coach is safe, the coachee is safe, and all others are safe. If there are any "disclosures," either party has a legal responsibility to share the information and to follow the protocol set out by the most current government guidelines.

## TO ESTABLISH A POSITIVE WORKING RELATIONSHIP BETWEEN THE COACH AND COACHEE

The coach needs to be professional and diplomatic in their approach, as well as warm and friendly. They need to be trusting, caring, and respectful. The quality of the working relationship will have a direct impact on the process (Parsloe and Wray, 2000:165). It is the responsibility of the coach to establish and maintain these qualities.

## TO LISTEN AND TO QUESTION SKILLFULLY

It is important for the coach to listen actively and to question skillfully (refer to Active Listening Skills and Socratic Questioning in chapter 4) in a professional manner. The coach needs to concentrate, not prejudge what is said, keep an open mind, and be aware of body language, personal space, tone of voice, and manner. Open-ended questions allow the coachee the opportunity to explore and reflect on their own situations and experiences. This will enhance the development of the coachee's critical thinking.

## TO OBSERVE CAREFULLY

In classroom observations, it is important for the coach to assume an unobtrusive role and be a non-participant observer. They need to be aware that their presence may affect those in the classroom. Classroom dynamics are powerful, and there may be a lot going on within that dynamics that the coach is not aware of. It is important that the coach focuses their attention during each observation as requested by the coachee and records accordingly.

## TO BUILD ON POSITIVES THE COACHEE ALREADY POSSESSES

The coach's aim is to help the coachee recognize first what they can do and what is successful for them, to believe in their own abilities, to reflect on an area of difficulty in order to set a goal, and to explore new ways of problem-solving. (Refer to notes on Pygmalion Effect in chapter 4.)

At the end of the coaching process, a previous coachee commented: "Beforehand, I was not conscious of what I was doing successfully. Your questioning helped me to realize that. It highlighted what I was doing right. It made me feel more positive. I give more praise to the students now too."

## TO FACILITATE THE CHANGE THE COACHEE DESIRES

It is important that the coachee is in control of the process and that they feel they are in control. They will identify their own area of concern and set their own goals. It is the coachee's contribution which is the starting point for coaching, "not what the coach thinks the coachee should learn or do" (De Haan and Burger, 2005:29).

Socratic questioning will help the coachee analyze what is happening, to explore new ideas, to plan, and to try again. The coach's role is to facilitate the process and to support and motivate the coachee to develop further skills. Changes are likely to be "incremental, very small yet significant differences" (Hook and Vass, 2002:18).

## TO HELP THE COACHEE FIND THE SKILLS TO SUSTAIN THAT CHANGE

To sustain change will require success at making change. Success breeds success. By increasing the coachee's self-confidence and self-esteem, it is more likely they will feel empowered to continue their growth throughout the process. Sustaining change is a "commitment to a lifetime of sustained reflection" (Proefriedt, 1994:18) and encourages teachers to continue to work and support each other.

## TO RECOGNIZE, AS A COACH, THAT ONE CAN LEARN FROM THIS PROCESS AS WELL

Coaches themselves find the process stimulating and helpful in their own learning and development. "To describe the situation as a two-way process is almost to understate the case" (Parsloe and Wray, 2000:148). "Seeing through the eyes" of another teacher will teach the coach about another's journey, as well as one's own. A coach's own critical thinking will improve. And the more reflective and self-aware a coach is, the more effective they are as a coach themselves (Rhodes et al., 2004:43). This is one of the many benefits of a peer coaching model and the opportunity for role reversal.

*Chapter 6*

# Possible Ideas for Coaching

A coachee will, undoubtedly, have his/her own ideas about his/her goals and what he/she wants to achieve through the coaching process. It may involve an area of knowledge, a teaching technique, a skill, an outcome, a particular class, a group of students, an individual student, and so on. It may be someone who regularly achieves "good" in their lesson observations and wants to achieve "outstanding"; or who achieves "satisfactory" and is aiming for "good." This chapter lists some ideas that may help refine some of those thoughts or give additional ideas.

"Change usually occurs small steps at a time. Small, incremental steps can make significant differences" (Hook and Vass, 2002:18).

*Teaching is an art.* And, as such, it is truly skillful. A true professional makes teaching look easy when, in fact, it is not at all. Teaching is multifaceted with many different talents, qualities and features.

Teaching can be seen as having four main and equal parts and a teacher needs to be successful in each of these areas as shown in figure 6.1.

If there is a piece of this puzzle missing, then a teacher will struggle. No one knows everything about their profession. We are all able to learn new skills and to grow, no matter how long we have been doing the job.

## KNOW SUBJECT MATERIAL

Many qualified teachers have a university degree in a particular subject area but often teach other subject areas. Also, a teacher may need help with learning new material. Curriculum changes happen frequently, so a new course or new subject may be introduced to the school, year group, or class. There

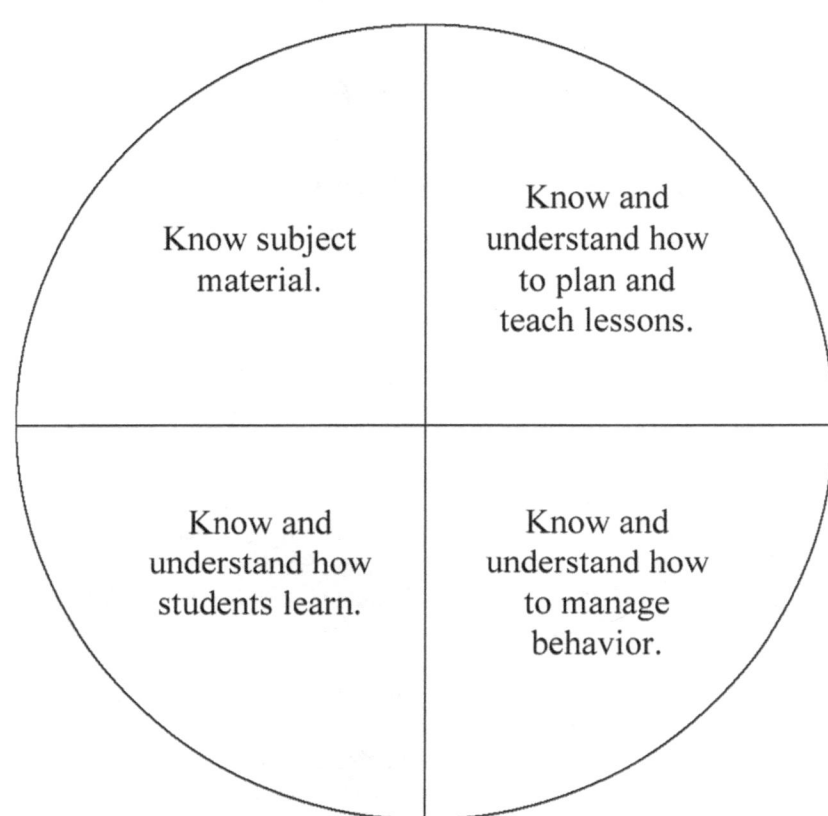

**Figure 6.1.** A Model of a Successful Teacher.

will be information which is given by the government, online, examination boards, teacher training days, and so on. Assistance may be needed to give additional support and clarification.

## KNOW AND UNDERSTAND HOW TO PLAN AND TEACH LESSONS

It is important for a teacher to structure and plan a series of lessons. Help may be needed for lesson starters, as the beginning of the lesson should be clear and have objectives set for the class to see and understand. Instruction and discussion should involve the whole class. The teacher may want to consider the pace of the lesson, maintaining a stimulating lesson, keeping students on-task, being able to answer student's questions without ignoring others, and setting appropriate homework where applicable. Lessons need a definite ending, as in a plenary, to link the lesson's objectives with the work completed. Classroom organization is important; it helps maintain the flow of the lesson and gives a positive working environment. If the teacher, the students, and the classroom are well organized, it reduces time being wasted, reduces frustration, aids teaching, and maintains a calm atmosphere for everyone (Gildner, 2001:63–73).

## KNOW AND UNDERSTAND HOW STUDENTS LEARN

The teacher needs to be aware of students' educational needs and to incorporate different learning styles into the activities of the lesson, such as those for visual, auditory, and kinesthetic learners. Where appropriate, it is important that the work is differentiated. Teaching individual students is necessary to help students learn and to keep them on-task but without ignoring the rest of the class. If a student has a specific learning need then professional advice is generally sought and recommendations given.

## KNOW AND UNDERSTAND HOW TO MANAGE BEHAVIOR

What is taught and how it is taught in a lesson is "a crucial element in the patterns of behavior which develop in the classroom" (Watkins and Wagner, 2000:79). Where the quality of teaching is high, behavior management problems are greatly reduced. However, students have individual needs and are affected by what happens outside the classroom, outside the school, and in their family life. Classroom dynamics and relationships within the class are powerful.

If a student has a specific behavior need then professional advice is generally sought and recommendations given. Getting to know students' names, getting to know them as individuals, having a seating chart, showing respect, giving praise, using positive language, catching students being on-task, all help to encourage learning and establish and develop positive relationships in the classroom. Establishing and maintaining classroom rules and routines in a consistent, firm, and gentle manner is also important in managing behavior.

The importance of preventing poor behavior cannot be stressed enough:

> The action which teachers took *in response* to a discipline problem had no consistent relationship with managerial success in the classroom. However, what teachers did *before* misbehavior occurred was shown to be crucial in achieving

success, through a preventive focus which reduced difficulty. (Kounin, 1977, cited in Watkins and Wagner, 2000:60–61)

## ADDITIONAL IDEAS

Other areas for coaching may involve work outside of the classroom. This may include the below:

- Leading staff/team meetings
- Leading training sessions
- Parent meetings
- Professional meetings
- Presentations

This peer coaching model is adaptable, so the list is inexhaustible!

*Chapter 7*

# Getting Started

It is important that the peer coaching model is as successful as possible. As a school or department, you may want to "start small" by introducing the model to a small number of staff. Allow staff to read and discuss the model. Allow volunteers to come forward and pairings to form. It is important to note that success relies on two people who can work well together. This was reinforced by the teachers who took part in the pilot. The following sections outline the steps and process. Once the information has been read and the teachers are ready, the coaching can take place.

Following the peer coaching, allow discussion about general outcomes and how to further develop it.

Some schools already use coaching models as a means of professional development.

If you and your school are already involved in coaching, then this peer coaching model can be included in the menu of styles and used where appropriate. It is time-efficient and cost-effective.

## Chapter 8

# The Process

*Reminder:* The actual process of this peer coaching model does not sit in isolation of everything else that has been described. Once the background information has been read by both participants, understood, discussed, and absorbed, then the practical side of the coaching process can begin.

After two teachers have paired up, they then need time to carefully consider their goal/focus (refer to chapter 6, Possible Ideas for Coaching). This is driven by individual needs. A decision is agreed concerning who will first take on the role of coach or coachee. An initial interview can then be set up and arranged between the two teachers.

The coach will need to have this book at hand, throughout the coaching process, in order to refer and refresh one's memory about the important coaching skills and key concepts needed to facilitate the process. The relevant pages can be referred to again and again, as needed.

The process includes the below:

- **Initial interview**
- **Observation and follow-up meeting**
- **Repeat observation and follow-up meeting as many times as the coachee wishes/needs in order to achieve their goal/focus. Their own scoring will indicate when this happens.**
- **Reflections**

The coach ensures that the coachee is given a copy of the paperwork immediately following each of the interviews, follow-up meetings, and observations.

It is also recommended that each participant keeps his/her paperwork together in their own file/folder for future reference.

Again, there are no secrets between the coach and coachee. Both are open and honest with each other about the process.

Roles are swapped between coach and coachee, and the process is repeated.

*Chapter 9*

# Initial Interview

The purpose of the initial interview is for introductions, for the coach to record background and current information, to acknowledge the coachee's goal/focus, to set up an observation and a follow-up meeting, and to answer any of the coachee's questions/concerns. (Refer to notes on How Adults Learn in chapter 4.)

## Chapter 9

## PEER COACHING

### Initial Interview

(Refer to chapter 5, notes on Key Concepts within This Peer Coaching Framework.)

### Introductions

- Discuss an overview of the process.
- Ensure both participants are volunteers.
- Confirm confidentiality as previously described.
- Confirm process is led and owned by the coachee.
- Offer observations as the coachee directs according to their wishes of classes/students, focus, and frequency.

### Interview

School:

Date:

Time:

Coachee:

Coach:

List successes coachee identifies as currently having. (Question and probe coachee. Refer to chapter 4, notes on Active Listening Skills, Socratic Questioning, Pygmalion Effect, Johari Window. Coach can continue writing on the reverse of sheet.)

Goal/focus as identified by the coachee. Include class/subject. (Refer to chapter 6, notes on Possible Ideas for Coaching. The goal/focus should be achievable, realistic, manageable.)

On a scale of 0 to 10 (0=worst, 10=best), where does the coachee see things now in relation to the goal/focus? (Refer to chapter 4, notes on Scaling.)

What makes it that number? Describe in detail.

Where would the coachee like the number on the scale to be?
What would that look like? Describe in detail.

What would students and staff notice when the goal/focus was achieved? Describe in detail.

Any other comments/information?

Coach and coachee arrange for an **Observation** and **Follow-up Meeting** based on the coachee's goal/focus. If needed, it is important that the coachee provides a class seating chart for the coach prior to the observation as it is unlikely the coach will know all the students in the class. This will help both parties with the discussion afterward.

Following the observation, the coach will need some time to reflect and prepare for the follow-up meeting, so there should be a gap of about an hour. The follow-up meeting should be held on the same day as the observation; otherwise, important information will be lost and forgotten. It is important that the observation and follow-up meeting are arranged at the end of the initial interview as other commitments can quickly take precedence.

The coach copies and shares all paperwork with the coachee.

## Observation (with Seating Chart Provided by the Coachee)
Date:

Time/length of observation:

Class/subject:

## Follow-up Meeting
Date:

Time:

Place:

*Chapter 10*

# Observation

The coach now prepares for the observation. There are sample observation sheets provided; however, it is important that the observation sheet matches the needs of the goal/focus of the coachee; otherwise, the relevant information will not be collected and time will be wasted. The coach may need to design an observation sheet that is "fit for purpose." Also, it is helpful to have a few sheets of plain paper available to add additional notes during the observation.

*Chapter 10*

## PEER COACHING

### Observation

It is important that the initial information is recorded below before the observation has begun to ensure clarity and avoid wasting time.

School:

Date:

Coachee:

Coach:

Class/subject:

Time/length of observation:

Seating chart provided: Yes/no

In-class support: Yes/no

Goal/focus (from initial interview):

Initial score (from initial interview):
Target score:

**Table 10.1.**

| Time | Notes |
|------|-------|
|      |       |
|      |       |
|      |       |
|      |       |
|      |       |
|      |       |
|      |       |
|      |       |
|      |       |
|      |       |
|      |       |
|      |       |
|      |       |
|      |       |
|      |       |
|      |       |

*Chapter 10*

## PEER COACHING

### Observation

This proforma is to be used as a cover sheet for the following observation sheets or an individually designed observation sheet. It is important that the information is recorded below before the observation has begun to ensure clarity and avoid wasting time.

School:

Date:

Coachee:

Coach:

Class/subject:

Time/length of observation:

Seating chart provided: Yes/no

In-class support: Yes/no

Goal/focus (from initial interview):


Initial score (from initial interview):
Target score:

## Observation

Purpose: To collect the teacher's frequency of positive/negative responses and examples observed.

**Table 10.2.**

|  | Verbal responses (Tally chart and examples of verbal responses below.) | Nonverbal responses (Tally chart and examples of nonverbal responses below.) |
|---|---|---|
| **Positive comments** | | |
| **Negative comments** | | |
| **Negative comments done in a positive way** | | |

## Observation

Purpose: To collect the frequency and types of on-task or off-task behaviors of a particular student, at regular intervals of two minutes, within a given time frame.

**Table 10.3.**

|  | On-task (Tick) | Off-task (Tick) | Note type of behavior. |
|---|---|---|---|
| 0 minutes | | | |
| 2 minutes | | | |
| 4 minutes | | | |
| 6 minutes | | | |
| 8 minutes | | | |
| 10 minutes | | | |
| 12 minutes | | | |
| 14 minutes | | | |
| 16 minutes | | | |
| 18 minutes | | | |
| 20 minutes | | | |
| 22 minutes | | | |
| 24 minutes | | | |
| 26 minutes | | | |

*Chapter 11*

# Follow-up Meeting

It is important that the coach takes some time to reflect on the observation *before* the follow-up meeting by rereading their notes and adding to them where necessary.

He/she will also use the time to summarize successes and difficulties observed, and to consider possible strategies in order for the coachee to make progress. These notes are written initially on a separate plain paper. Through careful questioning by the coach, the expectation is that the coachee will be able to identify their own successes, difficulties, and strategies. (Refer to chapter 4, notes on Active Listening Skills, Socratic Questioning, Pygmalion Effect, and Johari Window.)

The purpose of this peer coaching model is not for the coach to have the answers. As explained earlier, it is about the coachee becoming increasingly critically reflective in order to solve his/her own classroom issues with the support and careful questioning of a coach.

## PEER COACHING

**Follow-up Meeting**

School:

Date:

Time:

Coachee:

Coach:

Class/subject:

Goal/focus (from initial interview):

Initial score (from initial interview):
Target score:

## Follow-up Meeting

Score (given by the coachee based on lesson observed with goal/focus in mind):

Successes identified by the coachee. (Question and probe coachee. Refer to chapter 4, notes on Active Listening Skills, Socratic Questioning, Pygmalion Effect, and Johari Window. This is about the coachee being able to identify and support their current score.)

Any additional successes identified by the coach:

Difficulties identified by the coachee:

Any additional difficulties identified by the coach:

Coachee identifies additional strategies that can be implemented in order to improve their current score:

Coach identifies any additional strategies that can be implemented:

Any other comments/information:

Coach confirms he/she will copy and share notes of the follow-up meeting.

Arrange the next observation and follow-up meeting. The purpose is to continue with the observation and follow-up meeting cycle until the coachee feels confident that they have achieved their goal/focus. The process of scaling will indicate when this has been reached.

## Observation (with Seating Chart Provided by the Coachee)
Date:

Time/length of observation:

Class/subject:

## Follow-up Meeting
Date:

Time:

Place:

Once the coachee is confident that their goal/focus has been met, and their scaling indicates such, then it is the opportunity for the coach and coachee to switch roles. The process will begin again, in the same manner.

Alternatively, the coach and coachee can work in parallel, coaching and being coached simultaneously. The decision for this is with the coach and coachee as it depends on time, flexibility, and organization. In this situation, it would be best suited if both teachers had their own copy of this manual.

*Chapter 12*

# Next Steps

As mentioned at the start, it is important to realize that, as teachers, we are continuously learning. Therefore, it is important to see peer coaching as a positive experience, as a "tool" to our own learning and to honing our skills in a safe environment.

Once the cycle of peer coaching has completed, it is important for both participants to take time to reflect on their roles as coach and coachee. The final stage is "**Reflections**." It is very important that this stage is not omitted. It encourages those who have taken part to reflect on their respective roles, to consider at least three things they will do as result of their peer coaching, and to include any additional notes, thoughts, or ideas they may want to record. It is the decision of those who have taken part if they wish to share their reflections with one another. As mentioned previously, it is also recommended that each participant retains their set of paperwork in their own file/folder for future reference.

Finally, it is up to the participants when they return to the process of peer coaching. If one of the teachers would like more peer coaching than the other, that can be discussed and arranged within their pairing. The process can be repeated at any time with the same pairings, new pairings, in the same department or with different departments, from the same school or with different schools, as needs arise. That is the essence of this peer coaching model; it is driven by the coachee, as and when needs arise, being completely voluntary and confidential.

Staff may want to discuss the features of this peer coaching model, the process, and the benefits, formally or informally, with each other. It is an opportunity for the school to add this model to their menu of support for the professional development of its teachers.

The process of coaching encourages self-coaching. It increases critical thinking and encourages teachers to increase their awareness of being self-reflective. This leads staff to look more objectively at the situations they are in and to increase their skills for problem-solving. The end result will be improved teaching and learning.

## PEER COACHING

# Reflections

Reflecting on my experience as a coach or coachee, three things I will do as a result of the peer coaching:

**Table 12.1.**

Additional notes, thoughts, or ideas:

**Table 12.2.**

Name _____

Date _____

*Chapter 13*

# Case Study A

### INTRODUCTION

Kate and Hannah have paired up for peer coaching. Both currently teach Early Years Foundation Stage (EYFS) and teach classes of four- to five-year-olds at a primary school. Their classrooms are next door to one another. They work together on their long-term and medium-term planning but do their own short-term planning for their individual classes.

Coachee: Kate
Coach: Hannah

Kate's goal/focus:

- To manage dealing with difficult parents.
- I feel I can get too agitated and affected by parents and their insignificant behavior and comments.

Her own initial score: 6 (out of 10)
Target score: 8

*Chapter 13*

## PEER COACHING

### Initial Interview

(Refer to chapter 5, notes on Key Concepts within This Peer Coaching Framework.)

### Introductions

- Discuss an overview of the process.
- Ensure both participants are volunteers.
- Confirm confidentiality as previously described.
- Confirm process is led and owned by the coachee.
- Offer observations as the coachee directs according to their wishes of classes/students, focus, and frequency.

### Interview

School: *Primary School*
Date: *2nd March*
Time: *10 AM*
Coachee: *Kate*
Coach: *Hannah*

List successes coachee identifies as currently having. (Question and probe coachee. Refer to chapter 4, notes on Active Listening Skills, Socratic Questioning, Pygmalion Effect, and Johari Window. Coach can continue writing on the reverse of sheet.)

- *Kate puts her "all" into teaching the children.*
- *As a school, and led by Kate, we do lots of parent awareness, blogs, meetings, sharing.*
- *She takes concerns on board and supports where she can or needed.*
- *Kate invites parents in immediately if she feels she needs to give them more time.*

## Case Study A

Goal/focus as identified by the coachee. Include class/subject. (Refer to chapter 6, notes on Possible Ideas for Coaching. The goal/focus should be achievable, realistic, manageable.)

*To manage dealing with difficult parents.*

On a scale of 0 to 10 (0=worst, 10=best), where does the coachee see things now in relation to the goal/focus? (Refer to chapter 4, notes on Scaling.)
  *6*

What makes it that number? Describe in detail.

- *Kate feels she is a bit reactive to certain scenarios.*
- *She already feels it is an area she is concentrating on as it occurs frequently.*
- *She is able to discuss areas that affect children's learning but needs to fend off the more insignificant comments from parents.*

Where would the coachee like the number on the scale to be?
  *8*

What would that look like? Describe in detail.

- *Think before speaking.*
- *Take a little time and gather thoughts.*
- *Create opportunities to meet later rather than discussing instantly.*

What would students and staff notice when the goal/focus was achieved? Describe in detail.

- *Staff would notice Kate taking a little time before she responds to parents.*
- *A calmer approach.*
- *Children would see a change in their parents' interaction with the school.*

Any other comments/information?

Coach and coachee arrange for an **Observation** and **Follow-up Meeting** based on the coachee's goal/focus. If needed, it is important that the coachee provides a class seating chart for the coach prior to the observation as it is unlikely the coach will know all the students in the class. This will help both parties with the discussion afterward.

Following the observation, the coach will need some time to reflect and prepare for the follow-up meeting, so there should be a gap of about an hour. The follow-up meeting should be held on the same day as the observation; otherwise, important information will be lost and forgotten. It is important that the observation and follow-up meeting are arranged at the end of the initial interview as other commitments can quickly take precedent.

The coach copies and shares all paperwork with the coachee.

## Observation (with Seating Chart Provided by the Coachee)

Date: *7th March*
Time/length of observation: *20 minutes*
Class/subject: *Reception Class/Parent Meeting*

## Follow-up Meeting

Date: *7th March*
Time: *4 PM*
Place: *Classroom*

# PEER COACHING

## Observation

It is important that the initial information is recorded below before the observation is begun to ensure clarity and avoid wasting time.

School: *Primary School*
Date: *7th March*
Coachee: *Kate*
Coach: *Hannah*
Class/subject: *Reception Class/Parent Meeting*
Time/length of observation: *20 minutes*
Seating chart provided: Yes/no *N/A*
In-class support: Yes/no *N/A*

Goal/focus (from initial interview):

*To manage dealing with difficult parents.*

Initial score (from initial interview): *6*    Target score: *8*

**Table 13.1.**

| Time | Notes |
|---|---|
| 3.20 PM | *Parents, child, and Kate sat in meeting room.*<br>*Parents had concerns about information being passed to them about activities in school.*<br>*Kate thought first, before listing all the ways we supply information to the parents so they are aware of what happens.*<br>*Parents were particularly concerned as they feel their child is unable to relay any information to them regarding the day.*<br>*Kate reiterated the ways in which we communicate with parents.*<br>*The parents had concerns around a situation that had occurred that the child had not understood, and they felt they had been misadvised and something had been said.*<br>*Kate explained that she had not said what they felt she had said.*<br>*Going forward, Kate would help to support the child in understanding individual circumstances. She encouraged parent communication in the home/school book. Parents asked for specific one-to-one communication with the child to help prepare him for different occurrences at school.* |

## PEER COACHING

### Follow-up Meeting

School: *Primary School*
Date: *7th March*
Time: *4 PM*
Coachee: *Kate*
Coach: *Hannah*
Class/subject: *Reception Class/Parent Meeting*


Goal/focus (from initial interview):

*To manage dealing with difficult parents.*


Initial score (from initial interview): *6*     Target score: *8*
Score (given by the coachee based on lesson observed with goal/focus in mind): *7*

Successes identified by the coachee. (Question and probe coachee. Refer to chapter 4, notes on Active Listening Skills, Socratic Questioning, Pygmalion Effect, and Johari Window. This is about the coachee being able to identify and support their current score.)

- *Kate did pause before thinking.*
- *Reiterated important points, that is, methods of communication.*
- *Asked for someone else (staff) to be present.*


Any additional successes identified by the coach:

- *Patient.*
- *Speaking calmly.*


Difficulties identified by the coachee:

- *Knowing that she'd done as much as one could.*

Any additional difficulties identified by the coach:

- *Knowing that difficult parents will find something else.*

Coachee identifies additional strategies that can be implemented in order to improve their current score:

- *Remembering not to react straight away.*
- *Put into perspective with bigger picture.*
- *Not focus on the negative.*

Coach identifies any additional strategies that can be implemented:

- *Take a breath when you come away.*

Any other comments/information:

Coach confirms that they will copy and share notes of the follow-up meeting.

Arrange the next observation and follow-up meeting. The purpose is to continue with the observation and follow-up meeting cycle until the coachee feels confident that they have achieved their goal/focus. The process of scaling will indicate when this has been reached.

## Observation (with Seating Chart Provided by the Coachee)

Date: *6th June*
Time: *Early morning*
Place: *Reception Class*

## Follow-up Meeting

Date: *12th June*
Time: *9.15 AM*
Place: *Staffroom*

Once the coachee is confident that their goal/focus has been met, and their scaling indicates such, then it is the opportunity for the coach and coachee to switch roles. The process will begin again, in the same manner.

Alternatively, the coach and coachee can work in parallel, coaching and being coached simultaneously. The decision for this is with the coach and coachee as it depends on time, flexibility, and organization. In this situation, both teachers would need to have their own copy of this manual.

## PEER COACHING

### Observation

It is important that the initial information is recorded below before the observation is begun to ensure clarity and avoid wasting time.

School: *Primary School*
Date: *6th June*
Coachee: *Kate*
Coach: *Hannah*
Class/subject: *Reception Class/Parent Meeting*
Time/length of observation: *First thing in the morning, as children arrive.*
Seating chart provided: Yes/no *N/A*
In-class support: Yes/no *N/A*

Goal/focus (from initial interview):

*To manage dealing with difficult parents.*

Initial score (from initial interview): *6*     Target score: *8*

**Table 13.2.**

| Time | Notes |
|---|---|
| 8.45 AM | Child is reluctant to enter school. |
| | Parent is provoking a reaction from Kate by picking child up, constantly making eye contact. |
| | Kate sees other children in, noting what is happening from afar, but not reacting. |
| | When the other children are in, Kate calmly goes out to greet the child, taking the child and bag, talking to the child about morning routine. |
| | Being firm but fair to parent, Kate demonstrates regular morning routine. |
| | Kate does not evoke lots of chat as not necessary but ensures parent sees child coming into school smoothly. |

## PEER COACHING

### Follow-up Meeting

School: *Primary School*
Date: *12th June*
Time: *9.15 AM*
Coachee: *Kate*
Coach: *Hannah*
Class/subject: *Reception Class/Parent Meeting*


Goal/focus (from initial interview):

*To manage dealing with difficult parents.*


Initial score (from initial interview): *6*     Target score: *8*
Score (given by the coachee based on lesson observed with goal/focus in mind): *8*

Successes identified by the coachee. (Question and probe coachee. Refer to chapter 4, notes on Active Listening Skills, Socratic Questioning, Pygmalion Effect, and Johari Window. This is about the coachee being able to identify and support their current score.)

- *Staying calm and focused.*
- *Not personally dwelling on it for rest of the day.*
- *Remembering that the focus is the child, not the parent.*


Any additional successes identified by the coach:

- *Being able to repeat the procedure again with child and parent next morning.*
- *Language clear for child.*


Difficulties identified by the coachee:

- *A repetitive, annoying situation.*

Any additional difficulties identified by the coach:

- *Parent will continue to be tricky throughout school.*

Coachee identifies additional strategies that can be implemented in order to improve their current score:

- *Acceptance that parent will not change so it's about how Kate manages her own mindset.*
- *Focus back on the children and the class.*

Coach identifies any additional strategies that can be implemented:

- *Kate can discuss the situation with her coach which allows her feelings to be managed better.*

Any other comments/information:

*This series of observations and follow-up meetings has now ended.*

Coach confirms that they will copy and share notes of the follow-up meeting.
Arrange the next observation and follow-up meeting. The purpose is to continue with the observation and follow-up meeting cycle until the coachee feels confident that they have achieved their goal/focus. The process of scaling will indicate when this has been reached.

## Observation (with Seating Chart Provided by the Coachee)

Date:
Time:
Place:

## Follow-up Meeting

Date:
Time:
Place:

Once the coachee is confident that their goal/focus has been met, and their scaling indicates such, then it is the opportunity for the coach and coachee to switch roles. The process will begin again, in the same manner.

Alternatively, the coach and coachee can work in parallel, coaching and being coached simultaneously. The decision for this is with the coach and coachee as it depends on time, flexibility, and organization. In this situation, both teachers would need to have their own copy of this manual.

## PEER COACHING

**Reflections**

Reflecting on my experience as a coach or coachee, three things I will do as a result of the peer coaching:

**Table 13.3.**

*To set an area to work on, personal to me/my teaching.*
*To approach the target in a positive way.*
*To continue to have open discussions with colleagues.*

Additional notes, thoughts, or ideas:

**Table 13.4.**

- *It is good to discuss regularly with colleagues.*
- *It is not always necessary to record formally.*
- *We have had **many** discussions during this process which we haven't recorded. It is still ongoing.*
- *I have learned quite a lot and I find the skills I am honing are transferable.*
- *This model is logical and easy to follow.*
- *Using the scaling process and having someone to talk it through help recognize the progress one is making.*
- *It has been very beneficial.*
- *It is adaptable.*
- ***Key** to its success is a good relationship between coach and coachee.*

Name: *Kate*
Date: *12th June*

*Chapter 14*

# Case Study B

## INTRODUCTION

Kate and Hannah have paired up for peer coaching. Both currently teach Early Years Foundation Stage (EYFS) and teach classes of four- to five-year-olds at a primary school. Their classrooms are next door to one another. They work together on their long-term and medium-term planning but do their own short-term planning for their individual classes.

Coachee: Hannah
Coach: Kate

Hannah's goal/focus:

- To extend children's learning through play, from **my** interaction with them.
- I am new to EYFS and feel this is an area to improve upon.

Her own initial score: 6 (out of 10)
Where she would like to be: 8

## Chapter 14

## PEER COACHING

### Initial Interview

(Refer to chapter 5, notes on Key Concepts within This Peer Coaching Framework.)

### Introductions

- Discuss an overview of the process.
- Ensure both participants are volunteers.
- Confirm confidentiality as previously described.
- Confirm process is led and owned by the coachee.
- Offer observations as the coachee directs according to their wishes of classes/students, focus, frequency.

### Interview

School: *Primary School*
Date: *2nd March*
Time: *10 AM*
Coachee: *Hannah*
Coach: *Kate*

List successes coachee identifies as currently having. (Question and probe coachee. Refer to chapter 4, notes on Active Listening Skills, Socratic Questioning, Pygmalion Effect, and Johari Window. Coach can continue writing on the reverse of sheet.)

- *I already learned **my** conversation is important and to follow children's lead/comment/questioning.*
- *I know sometimes **not** to intervene but to let the learning continue without adult input.*
- *I know it is important to scaffold learning.*

Goal/focus as identified by the coachee. Include class/subject. (Refer to chapter 6, notes on Possible Ideas for Coaching. The goal/focus should be achievable, realistic, and manageable.)

*To extend children's learning through play from **my** interactions with them.*

On a scale of 0 to 10 (0=worst, 10=best), where does the coachee see things now in relation to the goal/focus? (Refer to chapter 4, notes on Scaling.)
*6*

What makes it that number? Describe in detail.

- *I know what I need to do and am on my way, but I need to keep practicing and using the opportunities from the children.*
- *I must give **time** in the classroom to do this and raise its priority.*

Where would the coachee like the number on the scale to be?
*8*

What would that look like? Describe in detail.

- *Having confidence that I can move on children's learning through **their** play.*
- *And to do this through a variety of contexts.*

What would students and staff notice when the goal/focus was achieved? Describe in detail.

- *Staff would see improved lesson observations and interactions with the children.*
- *Children would notice I am playing more with them.*

Any other comments/information?

Coach and coachee arrange for an **Observation** and **Follow-up Meeting** based on the coachee's goal/focus. If needed, it is important that the coachee provides a class seating chart for the coach prior to the observation as it is unlikely the coach will know all the students in the class. This will help both parties with the discussion afterward.

Following the observation, the coach will need some time to reflect and prepare for the follow-up meeting, so there should be a gap of about an hour. The follow-up meeting should be held on the same day as the observation; otherwise, important information will be lost and forgotten. It is important that the observation and follow-up meeting are arranged at the end of the initial interview as other commitments can quickly take precedence.

The coach copies and shares all paperwork with the coachee.

## Observation (with Seating Chart Provided by the Coachee)

Date: *12th March*
Time/length of observation: *20 minutes*
Class/subject: *Independent Learning*

## Follow-up Meeting

Date: *12th March*
Time: *3.30 PM*
Place: *Classroom*

Case Study B

# PEER COACHING

## Observation

It is important that the initial information is recorded below before the observation is begun to ensure clarity and avoid wasting time.

School: *Primary School*
Date: *12th March*
Coachee: *Hannah*
Coach: *Kate*
Class/subject: *Independent Learning*
Time/length of observation: *1 PM, 20 minutes*
Seating chart provided: Yes/no *N/A*
In-class support: Yes/no *N/A*

Goal/focus (from initial interview):

> *To extend children's learning through play from **my** interactions with them.*

Initial score (from initial interview): *6*     Target score: *8*

**Table 14.1.**

| Time | Notes |
|---|---|
| 1 PM | Hannah is outside on the verandah with the children during independent learning. She is interacting with a group of 8 children using plastic drainpipes and cars, an activity they previously set up. She talked to them about what they were doing, what was happening, questioning "what's wrong"? Hannah was also supervising the class and dealt with behavior in other activities. |

## Chapter 14

# PEER COACHING

## Follow-up Meeting

School: *Primary School*
Date: *12th March*
Time: *3.30 PM*
Coachee: *Hannah*
Coach: *Kate*
Class/subject: *Independent Learning*


Goal/focus (from initial interview):

> To extend children's learning through play from **my** interactions with them.


Initial score (from initial interview): *6*     Target score: *8*

Score (given by the coachee based on lesson observed with goal/focus in mind): *7*

Successes identified by the coachee. (Question and probe coachee. Refer to chapter 4, notes on Active Listening Skills, Socratic Questioning, Pygmalion Effect, and Johari Window. This is about the coachee being able to identify and support their current score)

- *Using knowledge previously modeled by another teacher.*
- *Responding to what the children were doing and their own questions/ requests, for example, "Can we do this?" to extend for themselves.*


Any additional successes identified by the coach:

- *Interacting in **their** play and questions. Well done!*
- *Hannah used the children's ideas to extend their learning.*

Difficulties identified by the coachee:

- *Knowing where to take it next.*
- *How can I extend without changing the activity?*


Any additional difficulties identified by the coach:

- *It is difficult to extend in a group situation where there are lots of different children and ideas.*


Coachee identifies additional strategies that can be implemented in order to improve their current score:

- *Reading/researching for myself in books.*
- *Attend a course.*
- *Practice.*


Coach identifies any additional strategies that can be implemented:

- *Observe other staff.*


Any other comments/information:

Coach confirms that they will copy and share notes of the follow-up meeting.
Arrange the next observation and follow-up meeting. The purpose is to continue with the observation and follow-up meeting cycle until the coachee feels confident that they have achieved their goal/focus. The process of scaling will indicate when this has been reached.


## Observation (with Seating Chart Provided by the Coachee)

Date: *6th June*
Time: *10.30 AM*
Place: *Classroom*

## Follow-up Meeting

Date: *12th June*
Time: *9.15 AM*
Place: *Staffroom*

Once the coachee is confident that their goal/focus has been met, and their scaling indicates such, then it is the opportunity for the coach and coachee to switch roles. The process will begin again, in the same manner.

Alternatively, the coach and coachee can work in parallel, coaching and being coached simultaneously. The decision for this is with the coach and coachee as it depends on time, flexibility, and organization. In this situation, it would be best suited if both teachers had their own copy of this manual.

## PEER COACHING

## Observation

It is important that the initial information is recorded below before the observation is begun to ensure clarity and avoid wasting time.

School: *Primary School*
Date: *6th June*
Coachee: *Hannah*
Coach: *Kate*
Class/subject: *Independent Learning*
Time/length of observation: *11 AM, 20 minutes*
Seating chart provided: Yes/no *N/A*
In-class support: Yes/no *N/A*


Goal/focus (from initial interview):

*To extend children's learning through play, from **my** interaction with them.*


Initial score (from initial interview): *6*     Target score: *8*


**Table 14.2.**

| Time | Notes |
|---|---|
| 11 AM | *Children were playing "wolves."*<br>*Hannah was looking to extend learning, away from low-level role-play.*<br>*She took some children aside to ask/prompt storytelling skills.*<br>*Children were then able to extend learning.*<br>*Some to write stories.*<br>*Some to act them out.* |

# Chapter 14

# PEER COACHING

## Follow-up Meeting

School: *Primary School*
Date: *12th June*
Time: *9.15 AM*
Coachee: *Hannah*
Coach: *Kate*
Class/subject: *Independent Learning*


Goal/focus (from initial interview):

*To extend children's learning through play from **my** interaction with them.*


Initial score (from initial interview): *6*     Target score: *8*
Score (given by the coachee based on lesson observed with goal/focus in mind): *8*


Successes identified by the coachee. (Question and probe coachee. Refer to chapter 4, notes on Active Listening Skills, Socratic Questioning, Pygmalion Effect, and Johari Window. This is about the coachee being able to identify and support their current score.)

- *Quick thinking: How can I approach this?*
- *Stayed with children's ideas but extended learning through their storytelling.*
- *Pleased I could channel learning but not restrict their ideas.*


Any additional successes identified by the coach:

- *Took a risk as quite a difficult scenario!*


Difficulties identified by the coachee:

- *Tricky to engage some children.*
- *Would have liked more time for children to complete.*

Any additional difficulties identified by the coach:

Coachee identifies additional strategies that can be implemented in order to improve their current score:

- *More practice.*
- *Continue listening to the children.*
- *Consider: channeling ideas versus placing ideas.*

Coach identifies any additional strategies that can be implemented:

- *Extra practice.*
- *Seeing activities/ideas through.*
- *It is great to see adult involved in the play.*

Any other comments/information:

*This series of observations and follow-up meetings has now ended.*

Coach confirms that they will copy and share notes of the follow-up meeting.
Arrange the next observation and follow-up meeting. The purpose is to continue with the observation and follow-up meeting cycle until the coachee feels confident that they have achieved their goal/focus. The process of scaling will indicate when this has been reached.

## Observation (with Seating Chart Provided by the Coachee)

Date:
Time:
Place:

## Follow-up Meeting

Date:
Time:
Place:

Once the coachee is confident that their goal/focus has been met, and their scaling indicates such, then it is the opportunity for the coach and coachee to switch roles. The process will begin again, in the same manner.

Alternatively, the coach and coachee can work in parallel, coaching and being coached simultaneously. The decision for this is with the coach and coachee as it depends on time, flexibility, and organization. In this situation, both teachers would need to have their own copy of this manual.

*Case Study B*

## PEER COACHING

## Reflections

Reflecting on my experience as a coach or coachee, three things I will do as a result of the peer coaching:

**Table 14.3.**

*Continue to try different approaches with children to improve teaching.*
*Learn from times when it doesn't go to plan.*
*Listen to colleagues and watch.*

Additional notes, thoughts, or ideas:

**Table 14.4.**

- *To approach things positively and always have an open dialogue that informally supports at all times.*
- *This process of peer coaching has opened up a dialogue that never stops.*
- *It is very easy to follow.*
- *It is not too long. If it was too long I wouldn't want to do it.*
- *The theory scattered throughout has been helpful but not too much.*
- *I would use it again and recommend it to others.*
- *The process is "learning about yourself."*

Name: *Hannah*
Date: *12th June*

*Chapter 15*

# Case Study C

### INTRODUCTION

Tom and Steve have paired up for peer coaching. They currently teach English to eleven- to sixteen-year-olds at a secondary school. Both are experienced teachers. Steve was new to the school last year.

Coachee: Tom
Coach: Steve

Tom's goal/focus:

- To be more positive with my classes, especially 9Y (thirteen- to fourteen-year-olds) as they are able but can be a lively class. I feel like some lessons I am "nagging" them to quieten down and work. I want to turn that around. I want to praise them more.
- It is an important year with exams coming up, and I want to get the best from all the students.

His own initial score: 7 (out of 10)
Where he would like to be: 9

## Chapter 15

## PEER COACHING

### Initial Interview

(Refer to chapter 5, notes on Key Concepts within This Peer Coaching Framework.)

### Introductions

- Discuss an overview of the process.
- Ensure both participants are volunteers.
- Confirm confidentiality as previously described.
- Confirm process is led and owned by the coachee.
- Offer observations as the coachee directs according to their wishes of classes/students, focus, frequency.

### Interview

School: *Secondary School*
Date: *24th January*
Time: *3.30 PM*
Coachee: *Tom*
Coach: *Steve*

List successes coachee identifies as currently having. (Question and probe coachee. Refer to Chapter 4, notes on Active Listening Skills, Socratic Questioning, Pygmalion Effect, and Johari Window. Coach can continue writing on the reverse of sheet.)

- *I know the English topics I am teaching this year.*
- *I have my notes/plans from last year to refer to.*
- *I know it is important to be thorough as a teacher but also to develop good relationships with the students.*
- *The school has "rules and routine" which I follow.*

Goal/focus as identified by the coachee. Include class/subject. (Refer to chapter 6, notes on Possible Ideas for Coaching. The goal/focus should be achievable, realistic, and manageable.)
   *To be more positive with my classes, especially 9Y. I want to praise them more.*

## Case Study C

On a scale of 0 to 10 (0=worst, 10=best), where does the coachee see things now in relation to the goal/focus? (Refer to chapter 4, notes on Scaling.)
 7

What makes it that number? Describe in detail.

- *They're basically a good class but I feel I am having to "nag" them to keep them focused and on-task.*
- *I have a seating plan which I insist on.*
- *I know all their names which I use and I know that helps with good relationships.*
- *I meet them at the door as they enter.*
- *I have a pacy lesson and that keeps them busy.*

Where would the coachee like the number on the scale to be?
 9

What would that look like? Describe in detail.

- *I wouldn't have to remind them so often to get on with their work. They all know it is an important year with exams coming up so they would get the work done.*
- *Students would take more pride in their work.*
- *If they were more focused we'd all be happier—them and me!*

What would students and staff notice when the goal/focus was achieved? Describe in detail.

- *I guess I'd come across as being happier in the classroom.*
- *It would have a positive impact on my other classes too.*

Any other comments/information?

Coach and coachee arrange for an **Observation** and **Follow-up Meeting** based on the coachee's goal/focus. If needed, it is important that the coachee provides a class seating chart for the coach prior to the observation as it is unlikely the coach will know all the students in the class. This will help both parties with the discussion afterward.

Following the observation, the coach will need some time to reflect and prepare for the follow-up meeting, so there should be a gap of about an hour. The follow-up meeting should be held on the same day as the observation; otherwise, important information will be lost and forgotten. It is important that the observation and follow-up meeting are arranged at the end of the initial interview as other commitments can quickly take precedence.

The coach copies and shares all paperwork with the coachee.


## Observation (with Seating Chart Provided by the Coachee)

Date: *31st January*
Time/length of observation: *Lesson 1, 50 minutes*
Class/subject: *9Y/English*


## Follow-up Meeting

Date: *31st January*
Time: *3.30 PM*
Place: *Staffroom*

*Case Study C*

## PEER COACHING

### Observation

This proforma is to be used as a cover sheet for the following observation sheets or an individually designed observation sheet. It is important that the information is recorded below before the observation is begun to ensure clarity and avoid wasting time.

School: *Secondary School*
Date: *31st January*
Coachee: *Tom*
Coach: *Steve*
Class/subject: *9Y/English*
Time/length of observation: *Lesson 1, 50 minutes*
Seating chart provided: Yes/no *Yes*
In-class support: Yes/no *No*

Goal/focus (from initial interview):

*I want to be more positive with my classes, especially 9Y. I want to praise them more.*

Initial score (from initial interview): *7*     Target score: *9*

## Observation

Purpose: To collect the teacher's frequency of positive/negative responses and examples observed.

**Table 15.1.**

|  | Verbal responses (Tally chart and examples of verbal responses below.) | Nonverbal responses (Tally chart and examples of nonverbal responses below.) |
|---|---|---|
| **Positive comments** | Well done. ///// <br> Good. /// <br> Good try. /// <br> Good effort. // <br> Yes. //// <br> Lovely. // <br> Thanks. //// | Smile. /// <br> Nod. ///// <br> Thumbs up. // |
| **Negative comments** | No. / <br> Not quite there. /// <br> Don't do that. / | Frown. / <br> Shake head. // |
| **Negative comments done in a positive way** | Think again. // <br> Getting there. // <br> More ideas. /// <br> Nearly. / <br> Chair still, thanks. / <br> Almost. //// | "The look."// |

Case Study C

# PEER COACHING

## Follow-up Meeting

School: *Secondary School*
Date: *31st January*
Time: *3.30 PM*
Coachee: *Tom*
Coach: *Steve*
Class/subject: *9Y/English*

Goal/focus (from initial interview):

*To be more positive with my classes, especially 9Y. I want to praise them more.*

Initial score (from initial interview): 7     Target score: 9
Score (given by the coachee based on lesson observed with goal/focus in mind): 9

Successes identified by the coachee. (Question and probe coachee. Refer to chapter 4, notes on Active Listening Skills, Socratic Questioning, Pygmalion Effect, and Johari Window. This is about the coachee being able to identify and support their current score.)

- *I felt more positive going into the lesson.*
- *Once I had established my goal during the initial interview I found I was already incorporating more positive language in my teaching.*
- *If I am more positive, the students are more positive and focused.*
- *It is interesting for me to have this type of feedback from Steve's observation as it highlights what I am doing and that it is working.*

Any additional successes identified by the coach:

- *Tom delivered a good lesson.*
- *He was organized and knew what he was doing.*
- *The students responded well to the praise which was subtle, not "over the top."*

Difficulties identified by the coachee:

- *I want to continue to do more of the same.*

Any additional difficulties identified by the coach:

Coachee identifies additional strategies that can be implemented in order to improve their current score:

- *I want to continue to give more praise.*
- *I want to do it with all my classes.*
- *It feels like I am creating a new cycle of praise, and that I am getting more work from the class. I'm happier and I think they're happier too.*
- *Teaching can be grinding/tiring but it's fun too when things go well.*

Coach identifies any additional strategies that can be implemented:

- *Continue to reflect on what you're doing and how you're doing it.*

Any other comments/information:

*This series of observations and follow-up meetings has now ended.*

Coach confirms that they will copy and share notes of the follow-up meeting.

Arrange the next observation and follow-up meeting. The purpose is to continue with the observation and follow-up meeting cycle until the coachee feels confident that they have achieved their goal/focus. The process of scaling will indicate when this has been reached.

## Observation (with Seating Chart Provided by the Coachee)

Date:
Time:
Place:

## Follow-up Meeting

Date:
Time:
Place:


Once the coachee is confident that their goal/focus has been met, and their scaling indicates such, then it is the opportunity for the coach and coachee to switch roles. The process will begin again, in the same manner.

Alternatively, the coach and coachee can work in parallel, coaching and being coached simultaneously. The decision for this is with the coach and coachee as it depends on time, flexibility, and organization. In this situation, it would be best suited if both teachers had their own copy of this manual.

# Chapter 15

## PEER COACHING

## Reflections

Reflecting on my experience as a coach or coachee, three things I will do as a result of the peer coaching:

**Table 15.2.**

*To give more praise, verbally and nonverbally.*
*To be more positive regarding students' efforts.*
*To try and turn negative comments into a more positive approach so students don't feel discouraged. We are all learning—them and us!*

Additional notes, thoughts, or ideas:

**Table 15.3.**

- *This peer coaching has been a really good process.*
- *I particularly liked the careful questioning. It made me think.*
- *I have learned a lot about myself from both roles, coach and coachee.*
- *I didn't realize I was "self-coaching" but I guess I am.*
- *I feel I am more reflective about what I do and how I do it.*
- *It has been great working with Steve on this.*
- *I would do it again with Steve or another member of our department.*

Name: *Tom*
Date: *14th February*

*Chapter 16*

# Case Study D

## INTRODUCTION

Tom and Steve have paired up for peer coaching. They currently teach English to eleven- to sixteen-year-olds at a secondary school. Both are experienced teachers. Steve was new to the school last year.

Coachee: Steve
Coach: Tom

Steve's goal/focus:

- I am concerned about a group of boys in 7W (eleven- to twelve-year-olds). Jake, particularly, seems easily distracted and loses focus.
- I was new to the school last year and, of course, the Year 7s are new to us this year. Therefore, it is worth me getting to know them as best I can.

His own initial score: 6 (out of 10)
Where he would like to be: 9

## PEER COACHING

### Initial Interview

(Refer to chapter 5, notes on Key Concepts wthin This Peer Coaching Framework.)

### Introductions

- Discuss an overview of the process.
- Ensure both participants are volunteers.
- Confirm confidentiality as previously described.
- Confirm process is led and owned by the coachee.
- Offer observations as the coachee directs according to their wishes of classes/students, focus, and frequency.

### Interview

School: *Secondary School*
Date: *24th January*
Time: *3.30 PM*
Coachee: *Steve*
Coach: *Tom*

List successes coachee identifies as currently having. (Question and probe coachee. Refer to chapter 4, notes on Active Listening Skills, Socratic Questioning, Pygmalion Effect, and Johari Window. Coach can continue writing on the reverse of sheet.)

- *I gained promotion coming to a new job/new school last year.*
- *I have settled in and really like it as everyone is friendly and helpful.*
- *I like sharing my ideas with the department and learning about theirs.*
- *Students and parents are great too.*

Goal/focus as identified by the coachee. Include class/subject. (Refer to chapter 6, notes on Possible Ideas for Coaching. The goal/focus should be achievable, realistic, and manageable.)

> *To monitor/track Jake's behavior in class to see how he is responding and how I can improve things for him.*

On a scale of 0 to 10 (0=worst, 10=best), where does the coachee see things now in relation to the goal/focus? (Refer to chapter 4, notes on Scaling.)
*6*

What makes it that number? Describe in detail.

- *Jake always arrives to class on time.*
- *He is quiet. He seems to try in class but is slow getting his work completed.*
- *He is friendly with the other boys.*

Where would the coachee like the number on the scale to be?
*9*

What would that look like? Describe in detail.

- *As students are in ability setting for English I would like to see him complete the class work.*
- *Raise his hand when he has any questions.*
- *Offer answers and take part in discussions.*

What would students and staff notice when the goal/focus was achieved? Describe in detail.

- *I think Jake's confidence would improve and we'd all see him "grow."*
- *Perhaps we'd see it in other subject areas too.*

Any other comments/information?

Coach and coachee arrange for an **Observation** and **Follow-up Meeting** based on the coachee's goal/focus. If needed, it is important that the coachee provides a class seating chart for the coach prior to the observation as it is unlikely the coach will know all the students in the class. This will help both parties with the discussion afterward.

Following the observation, the coach will need some time to reflect and prepare for the follow-up meeting, so there should be a gap of about an hour.

The follow-up meeting should be held on the same day as the observation; otherwise, important information will be lost and forgotten. It is important that the observation and follow-up meeting are arranged at the end of the initial interview as other commitments can quickly take precedence.

The coach copies and shares all paperwork with the coachee.

## Observation (with Seating Chart Provided by the Coachee)

Date: *1st February*
Time/length of observation: *Lesson 3, 25 minutes, first half of lesson.*
Class/subject: *Jake in 7W/English*

## Follow-up Meeting

Date: *1st February*
Time: *3.30 PM*
Place: *Staffroom*

# PEER COACHING

## Observation

This proforma is to be used as a cover sheet for the following observation sheets or an individually designed observation sheet. It is important that the information is recorded below before the observation is begun to ensure clarity and avoid wasting time.

School: *Secondary School*
Date: *1st February*
Coachee: *Steve*
Coach: *Tom*
Class/subject: *Jake in 7W/English*
Time/length of observation: *Lesson 3, 25 minutes, first half of lesson*
Seating chart provided: Yes/no *Yes*
In-class support: Yes/no *No*

Goal/focus (from initial interview):

> *To monitor/track Jake's behavior in class to see how he is responding and how I can improve things for him.*

Initial score (from initial interview): *6*     Target score: *9*

## Observation

Purpose: To collect the frequency and types of on-task or off-task behaviors of a particular student, at regular intervals of 2 minutes, within a given time frame.

Table 16.1.

|  | On-task (Tick) | Off-task (Tick) | Note type of behavior |
|---|---|---|---|
| 0 minutes |  | X | Jake is talking to others. |
| 2 minutes | X |  | Getting things out of his bag. |
| 4 minutes |  | X | Fiddling with things on his desk. |
| 6 minutes | X |  | Listening to teaching points. |
| 8 minutes |  | X | Fiddling. |
| 10 minutes | X |  | Listening to teaching points. |
| 12 minutes | X |  | Listening to teaching points. |
| 14 minutes |  | X | Fiddling. |
| 16 minutes |  | X | Fiddling. |
| 18 minutes | X |  | Mr. S. talks to Jake, gives one-to-one help. |
| 20 minutes | X |  | Doing written work. |
| 22 minutes | X |  | Doing written work. |
| 24 minutes |  | X | Fiddling. |
| 26 minutes | X |  | Doing written work. |

*Case Study D*

# PEER COACHING

## Follow-up Meeting

School: *Secondary School*
Date: *1st February*
Time: *3.30 PM*
Coachee: *Steve*
Coach: *Tom*
Class/subject: *Jake in 7W/English*

Goal/focus (from initial interview):

> *To monitor/track Jake's behavior in class to see how he is responding and how I can improve things for him.*

Initial score (from initial interview): *6*   Target score: *9*

Score (given by the coachee based on lesson observed with goal/focus in mind): *7*

Successes identified by the coachee. (Question and probe coachee. Refer to chapter 4, notes on Active Listening Skills, Socratic Questioning, Pygmalion Effect, and Johari Window. This is about the coachee being able to identify and support their current score.)

- *I think Jake knew we were observing him.*
- *I have rearranged the seating in the class and I think that is helping.*
- *I am more aware of Jake and his friends so I am keeping a closer eye on him.*
- *It is interesting to see the actual tracking of Jake in class. I couldn't have collected that information on my own.*

Any additional successes identified by the coach:

- *Steve was giving one-to-one teaching to Jake.*
- *He had prepared his lesson.*
- *The students enjoyed what they were doing.*

Difficulties identified by the coachee:

- *I want Jake to be more focused so he completes the work in class. He is able enough.*

Any additional difficulties identified by the coach:

Coachee identifies additional strategies that can be implemented in order to improve their current score:

- *Talk to some of Jake's other teachers and see if they have the same problem and what they are doing to help Jake.*
- *Look through records/notes from Jake's previous school to see if there are any background issues or suggested strategies.*

Coach identifies any additional strategies that can be implemented:

- *Talk to Jake's Head of Year.*

Any other comments/information:

Coach confirms that they will copy and share notes of the follow-up meeting.
Arrange the next observation and follow-up meeting. The purpose is to continue with the observation and follow-up meeting cycle until the coachee feels confident that they have achieved their goal/focus. The process of scaling will indicate when this has been reached.

## Observation (with Seating Chart Provided by the Coachee)

Date: *8th February*
Time: *Lesson 3, 25 minutes, first half of lesson*
Place: *Room 6*

## Follow-up Meeting

Date: *8th February*
Time: *3.30 PM*
Place: *Staffroom*


Once the coachee is confident that their goal/focus has been met, and their scaling indicates such, then it is the opportunity for the coach and coachee to switch roles. The process will begin again, in the same manner.

Alternatively, the coach and coachee can work in parallel, coaching and being coached simultaneously. The decision for this is with the coach and coachee as it depends on time, flexibility, and organization. In this situation, it would be best suited if both teachers had their own copy of this manual.

## Chapter 16

# PEER COACHING

## Observation

This proforma is to be used as a cover sheet for the following observation sheets or an individually designed observation sheet. It is important that the information is recorded below before the observation is begun to ensure clarity and avoid wasting time.

School: *Secondary School*
Date: *8th February*
Coachee: *Steve*
Coach: *Tom*
Class/subject: *Jake in 7W/English*
Time/length of observation: *Lesson 3, 25 minutes, first half of lesson*
Seating chart provided: Yes/no *Yes*
In-class support: Yes/no *No*


Goal/focus (from initial interview):

> *To monitor/track Jake's behavior in class to see how he is responding and how I can improve things for him.*


Initial score (from initial interview): *6*     Target score: *9*

## Observation

Purpose: To collect the frequency and types of on-task or off-task behaviors of a particular student, at regular intervals of 2 minutes, within a given time frame.

Table 16.2.

|  | On-task (Tick) | Off-task (Tick) | Note type of behavior |
|---|---|---|---|
| 0 minutes |  | X | *Jake comes in talking.* |
| 2 minutes |  | X | *Gets things out of his bag and fiddles.* |
| 4 minutes | X |  | *Mr. S. gives Jake one to one, points to the board.* |
| 6 minutes | X |  | *Jake follows the work on the board.* |
| 8 minutes | X |  | *Mr. S. praises Jake and others.* |
| 10 minutes | X |  | *Jake is doing the written work.* |
| 12 minutes | X |  | *Jake is doing the written work.* |
| 14 minutes | X |  | *Class discussion, Jake is listening.* |
| 16 minutes | X |  | *Still listening.* |
| 18 minutes | X |  | *Jake offers an answer, is praised.* |
| 20 minutes | X |  | *Doing written work.* |
| 22 minutes |  | X | *Fiddling.* |
| 24 minutes | X |  | *Mr. S. walks past, doing written work.* |
| 26 minutes | X |  | *Doing written work.* |

Chapter 16

# PEER COACHING

## Follow-up Meeting

School: *Secondary School*
Date: *8th February*
Time: *3.30 PM*
Coachee: *Steve*
Coach: *Tom*
Class/subject: *Jake in 7W/English*


Goal/focus (from initial interview):

> *To monitor/track Jake's behavior in class to see how he is responding and how I can improve things for him.*


Initial score (from initial interview): *6*     Target score: *9*

Score (given by the coachee based on lesson observed with goal/focus in mind): *9*


Successes identified by the coachee. (Question and probe coachee. Refer to chapter 4, notes on Active Listening Skills, Socratic Questioning, Pygmalion Effect, and Johari Window. This is about the coachee being able to identify and support their current score.)

- *This lesson surpassed my expectations.*
- *I engaged with Jake at the beginning of the lesson and he stayed on-task.*
- *I recognize that Jake may always be one of the last ones to finish but I encourage him and that helps. His other teachers have said the same.*
- *I give frequent one-to-one support during the lesson. It is quick but it certainly helps.*
- *I keep my eye on him so a smile, nod help too.*


Any additional successes identified by the coach:

- *Everyone in the class seemed settled, was focused, worked.*

Difficulties identified by the coachee:

Any additional difficulties identified by the coach:

Coachee identifies additional strategies that can be implemented in order to improve their current score:

- *Share Jake's success in English with his parents at Open Evening which is coming up soon.*

Coach identifies any additional strategies that can be implemented:

Any other comments/information:

*This series of observations and follow-up meetings has now ended.*

Coach confirms that they will copy and share notes of the follow-up meeting.
Arrange the next observation and follow-up meeting. The purpose is to continue with the observation and follow-up meeting cycle until the coachee feels confident that they have achieved their goal/focus. The process of scaling will indicate when this has been reached.

## Observation (with Seating Chart Provided by the Coachee)

Date:
Time:
Place:

## Follow-up Meeting

Date:
Time:
Place:

Once the coachee is confident that their goal/focus has been met, and their scaling indicates such, then it is the opportunity for the coach and coachee to switch roles. The process will begin again, in the same manner.

Alternatively, the coach and coachee can work in parallel, coaching and being coached simultaneously. The decision for this is with the coach and coachee as it depends on time, flexibility, and organization. In this situation, it would be best suited if both teachers had their own copy of this manual.

*Case Study D*

# PEER COACHING

## Reflections

Reflecting on my experience as a coach or coachee, three things I will do as a result of the peer coaching:

**Table 16.3.**

*Get to know the students as individuals as quickly as I can.*
*Have a seating plan but if it isn't working be flexible and change it.*
*Give frequent one-to-one, however brief.*

Additional notes, thoughts, or ideas:

**Table 16.4.**

- *The coaching model is really good as I felt in control the whole time.*
- *The observations gave me information that I couldn't have gotten on my own.*
- *Tom and I said we'd use the coaching again as it helps us as teachers.*
- *The students must benefit from our coaching too!*

Name: *Steve*
Date: *14th February*

# References

Clutterbuck, D. and Megginson, D. (2005) *Making Coaching Work: Creating a coaching culture*. London: Chartered Institute of Personnel and Development.

The Coaching and Mentoring Network (2006) *'Everything You Ever Wanted to Know about Coaching and Mentoring, and Quite A Lot that You Probably Didn't'*. Retrieved from http://www.coachingnetwork.org.uk.

CUREE (2005) *'Mentoring and Coaching CPD Capacity Building Project'*, DfES National Framework for Mentoring and Coaching. Retrieved from http://www.curee.co.uk.

De Haan, E. and Burger, Y. (2005) *Coaching with Colleagues—An Action Guide for One-to-One Learning*. Basingstoke: Palgrave Macmillan.

Fiszer, E. (2004) *How Teachers Learn Best*. Maryland: Scarecrow Education.

George, E., Iveson, C. and Ratner, H. (2006) *Briefer—A Solution Focused Manual*. London: BT Press.

Gildner, C. (2001) *Enjoy Teaching—Helpful Hints for the Classroom*. London: Scarecrow Press.

Gottesman, B. (2000) *Peer Coaching for Educators*. Folkestone: Scarecrow Press.

Hook, P. and Vass, A. (2002) *Teaching with Influence*. London: David Fulton Publishers.

MacLennan, N. (1995) *Coaching and Mentoring*. Hampshire: Gower Publishing Limited.

Parsloe, E. and Wray, M. (2000) *Coaching and Mentoring—Practical Methods to Improve Learning*. London: Kogan Page.

Proefriedt, W.A. (1994) *How Teachers Learn—Toward a More Liberal Teacher Education*. New York: Teachers College Press.

Rhodes, C., Stokes, M. and Hampton, G. (2004) *A Practical Guide to Mentoring, Coaching and Peer-Networking*. London: Routledge Falmer.

Watkins, C. and Wagner, P. (2000) *Improving School Behaviour*. London: Paul Chapman Publishing.

West, N. (1998) *Middle Management in the Primary School- A Development Guide for Curriculum Leaders, Subject Managers and Senior Staff, Second Edition*. London: David Fulton Publishers.

Wikipedia (2006) *'Johari Window'*. Retrieved from http://en.wikipedia.org/wiki/Johari_window.

# Index

active listening skills, 4, 7, 8, 13, 14
attitude, 3–4, 5

coach, 1–2, 3–4
coachee, 5
coaching, 1–2, 5
coaching skills, 7–12

disclosures, 3, 14

effort, 3, 4

follow-up meeting, 23–24, 39, 40–43

how adults learn, 4, 7–8

initial interview, 23–24, 25, 26–29

Johari Window, 4, 7, 10–12

key concepts, 13–16

mentor, 1–2, 5–6
mentoring, 1–2, 5–6

observation, 23–24, 31, 32–37

peer coaching, 2, 5, 21, 23–24, 45–46
professional development, 21, 45–46
Pygmalion effect, 4, 7, 9–10, 15

reflections, 23–24, 45–46, 47–48

scaling, 4, 7, 10
self-coaching, 2, 46
skills, 3, 4
Socratic questioning, 4, 7, 8–9, 14

teaching, 17–20

# About the Author

**Lanette Bridgman**, MA, is a teacher with thirty-five years of experience in education. She was a classroom teacher for twenty-five years having taught five- to eleven-year-olds and undertook a variety of roles in US and UK schools. As a behavior specialist for ten years, she worked with eleven- to sixteen-year-olds and was an advisory teacher across a range of secondary schools in the UK. She is currently retired and lives with her husband near London, England.

www.ingramcontent.com/pod-product-compliance
Lightning Source LLC
Chambersburg PA
CBHW030145240426
43672CB00005B/282